how to be eaten by a lion

For Todd and Keith,

With thanks, I hope you
enjoy, and I hope I haven't
ruined poetry for you :)

Mike
6-12-2014

HOW TO BE EATEN BY A LION

MICHAEL JOHNSON

NIGHTWOOD EDITIONS | 2016

Nightwood Editions
P.O. Box 1779
Gibsons, BC VON 1VO
Canada
www.nightwoodeditions.com

COVER DESIGN & TYPOGRAPHY: Carleton Wilson

Nightwood Editions acknowledges financial support from the Government of Canada through the Canada Book Fund and the Canada Council for the Arts, and from the Province of British Columbia through the British Columbia Arts Council and the Book Publisher's Tax Credit.

This book has been produced on 100% post-consumer recycled, ancient-forest-free paper, processed chlorine-free and printed with vegetable-based dyes.

Printed and bound in Canada.

CIP data available from Library and Archives Canada.

ISBN 13: 978-0-88971-318-5
ISBN 10: 0-88971-318-9

for Stéf, mon amour

&

for my mother and father

CONTENTS

We are the song
death takes its own time
singing.

—Robert Hass

ORNITHOS

for Robert Wrigley

Sing of larksongs in the brambles and mud cities,
the Kivu lakeshore rookeries
along those cooled cradles of magma.
Sing the birthplace of death and drought,
of baobabs and jacaranda buds,
the stump-rumped waddle of dabchick
and duck, shag and scissorbill,
their heron wet cousins strutting rivers.
You brittle bastards—
lovebird, greenshank, tambourine dove,
tinkerbird, oxpecker, little leaflove—
you are great in your littleness,
your hover and yaw, the way you bleed
the light your bodies are made of.
We envy, we dream, we sun in your splendour,
the sky built into your bones.
O bird, bird of prey,
of prance and shimmer on the thermals.
Kingfisher, nightjar, swift and shrike,
honeyguide, harrier, curlew and crake,
coo and I will echo, telling my lips:
Go on, go on, these are your wings.

IN PRAISE OF PAIN

Fluent in dialects of mantis and chameleon,
we lay reading cloud hieroglyphs,
listening to insects gossip in the grass
beneath the largest nest we'd ever seen.
We believed beetles the ant-world gods,
all inkblot and iridescence and poise—
dung, rhino, stag—surely immortal.
But our friend's goliath had died that day.
Too out of its element, its rainforest home
where leopards whiskered the shadows.
No one mentioned loneliness.
The innumerable live, the rare die.
A million wasps, one less was not tragic.
So we visited that nest with stoic anger,
six kids with slingshots, six missiles, all true.
One cleft the papery hull and lit their rage.
Our second salvo plummeted the nest
to a *marakuja* thicket, were it emerged,
rolling, gathering momentum
toward the terraces and workwomen.
And we, watching, fired on. We anticipated pain
as they welled in a demented cloud.
Instead, they went to work on the women,
and followed them, screaming, to the creek.
And this one girl resurfaced—
the pastor's lessons fresh in her:
in *all* things praise Him—screaming praises
to the wasps, the pain, through her tears:
Bwana asifiwe! Praise the Lord.

VENGEANCE

They later called it *nyoka*—serpent—
a mamba no one had seen the equal of.
They skewered it with rebar and watched it writhe.
They began with delicious nonchalance,
laying bets on who would deliver the *coup de grâce.*
With slingshots and bearing balls
the boys inched up the tail break by bruise,
aiming short to spark and shrapnel in the gravel.
They loved quartz smoke like some vital ingredient
in the bread of vengeance.
Elders squatted, whittling blowgun arrows,
imploring everyone to not hasten this gift,
not cheat them of their rightful portion.
That is how he found them, the pastor.
He glared about, daring anyone
to question his compassion,
as he gripped the rebar, a piece he knew stolen,
and angered more, unplanted it
and bent as if to pick up the limp body
when it struck. Men beat it to pieces.
His hand burned, he said. He sank to his knees
while they ran for the campus nurse.
That was how he died, with his snake,
a creature who spoke the only language it knew.

IN PRAISE OF THE VILLAGE IDIOT

Torrents of sun from mica on the hedges,
the quartz driveways framed in avocados.
Babuleo and his anklebells long overdue.
Rumour has him in a new shirt, a jungle green.
Rumour has him radiant.
It will not last, for he's not what we want him to be.
He spies through windows, eats our garbage,
his testes dangling from torn shorts.
Someone's sure to get him new ones
because they can't handle his immodesty,
his seeming carelessness.
They don't realize he knows no other way.
He sucks clay because it tastes good,
a saltiness he's found nothing better than.
And his garbage meals shuck their ferment
to his delight—all tasting like gifts.

His anklebells sound his coming
and kids badger him where he goes.
He seethes and curses them,
their elusive ridicule, their cruel normality.
His gibberish is a longing, a palpable desire.
That he could speak such words,
find the right invective, some sweet slang.
Desire that he could just talk.
Then there are days—today perhaps—
when he finds a voice and sings,
a hollow rasping where his face speaks beauty,
blissful repose—a truce.
He makes fluent sense, a soulful parlance,
like Beethoven to his own deaf ear,
as though he's always spoken perfectly,
never said anything else, as though he, even now,
was just wondering: *Did I make music today?*

THE VOLCANOLOGIST'S LAMENT

Living things know the sound of their hour.
The stormchaser knows the wind calling,
the eye's silence before the hammerfall.
For the hellfighter, the sudden company
of fire, oil turned to tongues that lick the dust
with flame. For rockhounds the earth's

seismic bitchings, stones tumbling from Earth's
molten bruise. In all our hours
can one find more haunting a thrall than the dust
and shockwall closing over those calling
for help? Such images inevitably accompany
us into the grave: the fall

of lavasilk, magma's chaotic freefall
through the sky's strata to reclaim the earth.
A nightly pillar of fire to accompany
us, a pillar of cloud by day—what ashen hour
could pass without some stony lord calling
gravely from the depths? This sweet dust.

They say we are raised from dust.
The honey-heft of all the fruit fallen
in the orchards, the soil calling
commands of ferment and rot, the earth
reclaiming all. Everything is the hour
of his supper. We are his company,

his very wine and bread. We are a company
of fools for mistaking the holiness of dust.
Land, property, certainly. Not an hour
of these passes unbartered in the rise and fall
of markets and monies, but the earth
goes unheard. That lithic heart calling

its pulse up through the plates, calling
its wrath through the faults: I keep company
with gods, why do you not listen? This earth
is such a terrible loneliness. Built of dust,
they say. I'm just a man, bound to fall.
Why care without another to share the hours?

O firestone, I've unearthed nothing. O enemy hour,
when comes calling my friend in the fall,
my company into the country of dust?

THE VOLCANOLOGIST'S LAMENT II

From the distress of the undressed—
unbedded rocks, tripped-over tree limbs—
scurrisome bugs and so-many-legged pedes
unhomed: life is in the running fight,
that telltale scatter of things driven to endure.
We all know the reaper's come-hither claw wag.
Without cipher, the flourish and thrall offers so little,
yet faced with lavasilk on the slopes, we stare.
What has the flame to offer?
Survival is luck and love of oneself,
timing, smarts, a pinch of learned-the-hard-way.
Lava can warm you with the heat of all it has burned.
What it gives, it has taken.

RAINMAKER

They called you in their need,
none believing in your ricketed
legs and bird bones, the desiccated
eagle head you carried.

You shook your lion-tail sceptre
at their quiet ridicule,
strutted your beads and spat the dark fuel
of your prayers into the fire.

After the thunder and cloudgrace,
were they tears on weathered faces
laughing their thanks? Did they
ever believe in you rainmaker—
or was it enough they cried, *Asante!*
Asante! and drank the water?

HOW TO BE EATEN BY A LION
for Claire Davis

If you hear the rush, the swish of mottled sand
and dust kicked up under the striving paws,
its cessation, falling into the sharp and brittle grass
like the tick of a tin roof under sun
or hint of rain that nightly wakes you,
try to stand your ground. Try not to scream,
for it devalues you. That tawny head and burled
mange, the flattened ears of its sleek engine
will seem only a blur, a shock, a shadow
across your neck that leaves you cold.
It may seem soft, barely a blow,
more like an exquisite giving
of yourself to the ground, made numb
by those eyes. It may be easier just to watch,
for fighting will only prolong things,
and you will have no time to notice the sky,
the texture of dust, what incredible leaves
the trees have. Instead, focus on your life,
its crimson liquor he grows drunk on.
Notice the way the red highlights his face,
how the snub nose is softened, the lips made fuller.
Notice his deft musculature, his rapture,
because in all of creation there is not art
to compare with such elegance, such simplicity.
Notice this and remember it,
this way in which you became beautiful
when you thought there was nothing more.

BONE LULLABIES

Everything that comes here to feed dies.
Mazuku, the tribes say. Evil wind.
Volcanic air gone glacial through dried creekbeds,
stoking the flora to life, drawing the grazers.
Gazelle and kudu racks bedeck the turreted anthills
like underlings for the elephant pharaohs.
Why here? Perhaps this was the way to die:
drawn by green in an otherwise wilderness,
following the guideposts of your family's bones.
You'd follow swifts snapping the dusk down,
bequeathing evening to night.
The stars might seem a paradise descending,
birdcage blueprints for the rungs of your torso,
each rib sunned and razed, your breaths housed there
so that as you rest your marrow rocks the beasts to bed.
The soil springs the veined calligraphy of leaves.
The birds dine on the ripe fruits of your eyes,
perched on your carriage staves, flapping
their prayers in the dust to eventide songs
that roam your bones long after sleep has come.

ROCKHOUND

Across the quarries stone rose as if spooked
from a nest, percussive across the tailing ponds.
Shrapnel on the well-house tin carried a fume
from the opened marrow of a stone,
essence akin to that buzz-build before a sneeze.
Among the clades, the topazes and Jacobins,
hermits, mangoes, coquettes, brilliants,
giants, mountain gems, bees and emeralds,
it could have been any hoverbird thrumming,
the way memory pulls it through a prism, languid,
mesmeric, its all-coloured shadow across the wall.
It wasn't our dusty hides, the way he paused
to eye us like marvellous flowers,
it was how clatter from a stormless sky
assured him our divinity, the rain turned to stone.
He side-glanced us, awesome, godly, and gone.
Now any pebble underfoot can throw the tumblers,
take me back there, leaning on my dad,
the wind playing with our hair,
his sweat on my arm like a seed of sun.

DEMOCRACY

Côte d'Ivoire

Dervishes and snakehusks blown
against the broken quills of grass
along the ditches like lost prayers,
and the gendarmes, come so quietly
into the holy place of your home.
There might be ink on your thumb.
They might even drop your body
back in front of your home to warn.
Or the limbo of makeshift morgues
and months for proper papers,
and though your family know
your face like a Braille poetry of hurt,
they cannot take your body home,
they cannot anoint you for the dust.
Your simple white shoes—where
the blood was caked, your wife
could only pay the rag of her grief
across your shoes until they shone.

DEATH BY LIGHTNING

The story went: Three men
crossing a field for home
were struck by lightning.
Nobody said: Imagine the bolt
shunting through, the pain.
Or perhaps they spoke of these
beyond earshot, the gossip
of searchers who found them,
toenails smouldering, torched
from toe to top, the kinetic ball
splitting their skulls deftly as an axe,
cleft right and left and left
to smoke in the ozone musk.
The earth stayed warm,
as if light and lightning
had gathered to roast and talk,
and toast the bones of passersby.
No one said: Imagine the smell—
not steak or broil but burnt carrion,
the soot of souls fuming in stride,
hurrying home to sup and drink
and hear tales of sons,
and hold them on a knee,
safe from any passing storm.

LUCKY

The Guinness Book number
is seven—the most anyone
has been struck by lightning.
Roy. A park ranger. I imagine
him tall, a slight curve
to his shoulders as if cocked
for the unexpected. Burns,
lost toenails, cuts from above.
He had his hair catch fire twice.
What hurts most is the note:
of his suicide years later,
after the woman he loved
rejected him. Scarred shoulder,
ankles that twitched and ached
at static and ozone, that musk
making his skin crawl—
what else but to be deserted?
a fingerprint in stone and dust,
returned—lucky, unlucky—
to this earth whose love
of our bones is all we know.

THUNDER EGGS

Amethyst, agate, quartz—core incubi,
rarified ejecta upheaved and washed
to dross on the streambed bottom,
dried to a troupe of forgettable boulders.
On a hunch, seeing a wink of crystal,
a spyhole into brute-skinned stone,
we broke some on their brothers
and burst stone confetti about our feet.
Perhaps it was written in their code
the skies would break with them,
perhaps these were the sky's own eggs,
for the clouds shattered and cowered us in a cave
where we knew this could not ever be undone:
no two pieces could ever be restored.
Then sun chased the storm headlong
down the country, and the gleaming bits warmed
till the birds pecked them up,
and bound for the troves of their roosts
took wing with the gems in their beaks
like feathers from some great tragedy.

IN PRAISE OF MUD

for Dennis Held

Let us recite those hymns the wind bansheed
in our ears when we still believed
in the church of earth, the god of mud.
Let us praise those anointing tongues—
the locals said *Inanyesha*. It is pouring,
that eveningsong, cloud wrath, rain.
And for the earth turned brown and slick,
the playground dervish of the world
turned joyous gutwrench on the mud slopes,
turned gibberish and glee, when all that mattered—
the horizon clamped in cumulus teeth,
the mood blown to misery—was the joy
we found on a hill, in the rain, sliding,
when all that mattered was our thanks.
Yes, let us open the mud book and pray.

MURDER

File on file, lone, and run down the wind in ragged packs,
they flew and tossed in a duskdervish,
the sky snarling over its birch bones
the congregation cawing their way westward
to the castlekeep of their rookery.

Where had the word lost this meaning?
Throats gossiping to the galleries,
preened in their gleaming regalia,
their days spent sundering garbage bags and composts
while citizens welled the streets.

Where had murder become a killing, a betrayal of communality?
What bereavement could have led to such confusion—
the forgetting of this sacred culmination?

Old forgotten troths and habits—
murder recalled them, restored them,
saved them in great clattering groves reminding us:
You are not this bustle, this too-busy brood.
You are not isolation.
You are crowds who have forgotten to come together—
O murder, share your legion pulses.
Lonely brother splay your wings. O sister, join us,
we who miss you so in the night's long visit.

DEW

Kindles in the cool grass,
and the night builds hoarfrost
like small cities of glass.

Dawn will spill across
these scattered
shadows like leaves of light.

A hummingbird
will sip a bluebell flute
of dew and go on burning.

Grass blade, feather blur,
light, everything—
we are all a kind of fire.

TREE OF LIFE

Vines purchased in its gnarls and knuckled bark
to seem, at a distance, the tree's verdant flesh.
Patriarch. Relic. Beholden to the wind's supple tethers,
the soil's fertile decree, still it quivered in the sun
and boasted its branches and held itself exalted.
Its secrets became the autumnal leaves that flicker
and wane, yellowed and aged, clattering
through the gilded windrows of grass.
Its secrets spread in the afterstorm—shorn,
laid open in welters of dust and rot-haunt
so long disguised by its flowering perfumes.
The gardeners paid their mute respects.
There amid the tattered brambles was the pulsing heart:
worms besotted with rot, churned in the upheaval
into a thing wholly animate and delirious with ruin.
Witnesses discerned in the roil of bird bones
jewelled into vine runners, of hare skulls knurled
by jackrat and vole claws, of shrivelled cocoons
and windblown snakehides like paper money
in the wake of some great theft—its wasted pageantry
revealed: a floral carapace which had whispered
fertile nothings and flowered coercions
that held the birds and arborists, its last definite hopes,
and even the gentle, longsuffering worms, at bay.

THE CHURCH OF A BARN'S SHADOW

Crude broods have dined on antique tires,
gnawed the seatleathers and nursed grease zerks,
have littered in fender tenements and marvelled
how a barn's silvered boards lithen in the sun,
old chrome feeding the shadows crumbs of light.

Ravages settle on the sweet patinas of people, yes,
as dust, through sun. What yaw, what blaze.
The years like starving visitors. Isn't this your town?
Midas grass scratches its back on the breeze,
fields bristle their hay-fume, everything fodder,

the humidors of barns laden with horsepuck,
clover and sweat like powdered amber.
Isn't this your smoulder? Nights redolent of petrol
like the transit of unburnt prayers, streetlight gospels
of chrome, fridaynightgoers all heady with hope.

Perhaps you were raised in the church of a barn's shadow
and work put its roots into you, your idea of home
all duskful in the gloaming. But no matter
what soffits and gables the wind nightly gnaws,
home always held a roof of sky, roof of stars.

And that wind came from where the birds dressed in rainbows
and preened on the hoods of rusty cars and old men clapped
and the señoritas zapateoed out to praise them
and the birds strutted and shook their fires
and watched the holy rooms of children's eyes burn.

THE CHURCH OF MY MOTHER'S HANDS

Let those brightest bits of fluff
not be from the little bird broken by the window,
not the one we buried with due sorrow,
but the last one, little nectarivore glanced off
the glass by my mother's flowers. Let them be
his brush with grace, breastplumes lost
before she held him in her calloused
palms, and when he was revived and ready,
opened the church of her hands.

THE CHURCH OF ROT

Born of filth and putrid perfume
and rarely mistaken for a blessing:
corpsemusk, fetid sump thirsting
beneath the trees, sink of rotting chaff,
sodden arms reclaiming the dead.
Here in the understory, the grey-green
wooded fog, the air's wet touch
leaves a rampant fertility on the skin.
No parley of echoes, no babble
of colour and silhouette,
but burnished rot and fungus
brewing return, brewing sludge
and silk mold, that heaven of decay,
where to fall is to be borne
into the rising, the risen.

THE CHURCH OF STEEL

Lathe, knurl, taper, thread: steel is god.
Oil-sheened, blade-burnt by the kerf
of the tool's carbide tooth,
see how the excess molts,
how the shavings rope and wobble:
the turned thing itself turned bewitching.
Shavings have scissored my palms,
worked straight through my hands,
made my skin a bloody bloom.
Yet I return to steel and emery cloth,
to lathed aluminum like razor lace,
to rust dust and drills and dies.
I play precision: hone, sink, buff, bore,
to see the coils sizzle and spin, knowing
my mastery is fleeting, and the cost—
these scars—simply offerings
to a god whose face I form.

THE CHURCH OF PURSLANE AND PRIMROSE

Soapberry boughs rasp a solitary song on the panes.
She has only died today, will not be found
till Sunday, five autumn afternoons.
They'll not notice her flowerbed's botanicure,
her chimney smokeless in the setting sun.
They'll see her empty church pew.
Where she was fixture she is now a monument
of air, an emptiness the size and shape of her.
She nurtured pansies, purslane and primrose,
apple and cherry trees that sated the birds.
Her sons mark the plaque on the church wall,
steads whose cost no one could explain.
What to say in memoriam
now that her hedges will root and migrate—
she was kind, her gardens were amazing?
What could you have said, yesterday,
when she needed no blossom, just a nod,
a kind call at her fretwork oak door
you'd been meaning to see so long?

THE HOROLOGIST'S LAMENT

Gone are the greasy axle splines
your father thumbed like pages

in the good book of labour, the aged
cedars from their cradlestones,

the nations who homed here—lost
like air in the mouths of clouds.

Gone the rusty bones of old gods
and gone the woodland ghosts.

Gone, to sound, instead of words,
when you nestle to Time's chest:

the lilt of childhood laughter burst
from his breast like startled birds.

HELL

No lake of fire, no, it is waking
to find a drunk driver took her years ago,
and the child, briefly, achingly, on a machine,
and every waking they die again.

Hell is her holding her belly in an ambulance,
who didn't wake, only believed she woke
in the growing dawn, birds just opening their throats,
their song spread into the waters of night like a stain.

Think of only believing you woke.
Where she felt a sunrise like a foundry of opals
and the tinder bones of suns, really
there was the wind-kept croon of winter
on housecorners, the sun gone raggedly
into the last leaves. No more dapple, no sway.

No one would know what toppled firewood
or rusting pail was growing small
and hunched to gnomes of snow.

No one would come in spring and see
between the willow boughs
the chime he hung of hollow reeds,
the whittled trinkets that look like his family
whose hands in a breeze come together.

HOW WATER WORKS

They used to speak of this garden
where fungus and flowers riddled the moss
and a waterfall feathered away.
The place ached with wetness.
That is how water works: frost-sheer
turns talus turns gravel turns silt.
It stokes detritus, entices slugs
to stem and stalk, leaf, limb and trunk,
spills into wombs of lichen and liquorice,
mistletoe and moss, builds flowers in the ruins.
This was the garden they spoke of,
lost, or made up: the mist, the talisman sun
not so much shining as echoing
into amphitheatres of bluebell and boneset,
rattlebox and widowmaker mushrooms.
Perhaps they lied about the place
boasting its pageantry of bloom.
And how that waterfall glassed everything
with mist turned to frost.
The wild lilac shone. Fiddleheads,
so prone to motion, obeyed no breeze.
In glossy nests, frozen birds
clutched their hatches, realization come
too late. Dusk moaned of too-heavy trees,
branch explosions, the headlong showers
of tinkle and ring, the water oblivious
to the ground it was forever bound for.

SAND

Spilled down the stone totem to tend the tombs
of nameless crustaceans, into the commonplace
of our lives, stolen from the beach to cushion
the walks, to silk, to soothe. You who were stone
once, royalty once, divinity in the molten dark—
you who were once immaculately conceived as glass.
Wrecked and washed in the blue blood of glaciers,
tomed in birchbone and cedarbough fed to kilns,
gone where none would grieve the sea's thievings,
high-piled in dune lees and windspun
from the crests and ridgebreaks like gritty tongues
telling the old, old tale of stone so long lost
it has forgotten where it came from, forgotten its name,
how it ever came to be desert.

THE BONE TEMPLE

At his craftbench he built bookends from the thin hips
of what once must have been a beautiful girl.
His blind monk exhumed the hand-maps

of lost lands written in brisket and casket-shard,
republics long fallen. Two bronzed skulls
pilastered like gatekeepers: enter, and be devoured

by the spirit. From a pedestal, a tarsaled fist
in boneful regalia pointed toward the pulpit.
Lattices across the vault, a fretwork trellis

up the wall of saints, rib shutters and shin grates
and carved in all: flowers, as if the bones had bloomed,
as if the place had conjured offering plates

of skulls and a chandelier of so many hundred hands
holding the light, of myths and bounty lists—
this garden growing bonemeal. What should a man

smell after breathing skeletons? Finishing
the last mosaic of teeth—welcome to the house of God—
he stopped. It was too much. Apparently nothing

had happened. These relics, these souls, had not died
slaves, not heard their kind dubbed spawn
of monkeys, progeny of sin, not been colonized

and spent like so many dirty bills, but were blessed, yea,
destined, to beautify this sanctuary, the dark transept,
the chancel where sunlight washed the shadows away.

IN THE KINGDOM OF AGONY

Perhaps you've seen that photo of him in the lotus
in a crowded intersection of Saigon, 1963.
His name is Thích Quảng Đức, but nobody cares,
they just see a congregation of monks, and notice
him beside a car parked with its hood up in the street.
They haven't registered what he's doing, just stare,

in disbelief, as he sets himself on fire.
This photo is infamous
for capturing what no one could ever say.
The print on my shelf holds no less power.
You can't tell what colour the sky is,
but you get this sensation the day

must've been the bluest he'd ever seen. You feel certain
he, until this day, this place,
had never seen sky so bright, clouds parted so perfectly.
Monks mourn seeing him showered in leaves of flame.
Wind fanning the billows leaves half his face
visible, and he, so quiet, seems to be sleeping peacefully

in the kingdom of agony. They say he was silent,
said *nothing*, soundless as the burn
burrowed in. In the heft of those first
seconds—wind gone in one moment
from kind to brutal, the flames a taste learned
the wrong way—you wonder if his life blurred

by: were his feet gentle to the earth each day?
Did he treat every little bird like a brother—did he live
right? And you realize he must've known: yes,
he had. His choice was an offering laid
in the street for everyone, and what he had to give
was his willingness to bathe in gas

knowing what was to come:
his domed head would peel and melt,
his lightly muscled calves, his fingers,
the familiar corded tendons of his hands, become
a bracken of ashes, a carbon twine of burnt
bones and sinew and papery skin blown to powder.

Yet he still set himself on fire. Imagine that:
controlling the muscles that had carried
you so far, down paths and monastery passages—
imagine how hard dropping a match
could be. He seems as if he's never been afraid,
as if the resolve and courage

gathered with his robes into his lap are gifts
he's been walking toward all his life. And that moment—
a recognizing of old friends, a convergence of straight
lines—that pure, indisputable point, is a gift,
so recognizable it needs no acknowledgement,
he just closes his eyes, speaks flame.

PARENTS WAITING FOR WAVES TO RETURN KIDS

Sri Lanka

You can see them on the beach most days
carrying some sandal, or toy, some flicker
sparked by flotsam, peering
as if a wave has just called their names.

They believe the waves have taken their kids
for some tour, and they must beacon
hope on the beach to guide them home.

The toll became the sum of a village
and the next, then a small island and those around—
the toll itself swept away from all footing.
Where could one find perspective?
What would it matter if the sum were everyone
you'd ever known, ever met, or just one?

Yesterday, the story goes, a man and his son
walked off a boat, home from a thousand miles
where the waves had taken and left them.

This new perspective terrorizes the lonely couples.
Not its remove from the new norm,
which forever includes the truth of the gulls
frantic above the sea foam gnawing
on houses, upending every known thing,
their rice pots steaming unladled, their bowls
in that manner of milk fired to glass
shattering, cars crumpled like toys...
all of these as common as breathing, dependable
as surf, how it gives, takes, gives back.

No, it is how if they had only held on, tighter,
they would know which beach
they were coming home from.

DEATH BY FORGETFULNESS

Let us call him Sonny.
Who could fault him the autumn gloom,
his first bottle in years?

His dogs not too hungry
there by the bumper,
he reacquainted himself with the bar.

Later, the highway turned canvas,
as if some demon from a distant pit
brushed those dogs behind Sonny's truck.

Dabs of colour, clots of hair.
Then full, bold strokes.
Past the stores in town,

by the welcome sign, to another bar.
There the familiar truck and the leashes
and remnants.

I could tell you how they beat him,
how he took so long to heal,
the bones in late winter like a psalm

of break and bruise, a haunt of fists,
how he never drove again.
You might pass his truck there for a time,

just a beater, seemingly left yesterday,
as if the owner could be anywhere
out walking his dogs.

HOW TO CARRY A CROSS
for John Dickinson

A professor once confided his many years in Japan,
how MI6 called on his expertise
to recommend suitable targets for some new weapon.
Knowing friends there, his great love of the region,
a loyal subject of The Crown,
he suggested Nagasaki and Hiroshima.

You can imagine whatever life you want for him.
Perhaps a bachelor, rumpled and worn
in that way stones grow further down the river—
a life given to teaching, to charity.
Perhaps he fluttered around a flame of scotch.

What life have you imagined for him?
Did you bless him with grandchildren, a home
unmolested by fire—have you dignified his temples
with grey, unruly, hairs his students loved
for the way they tufted out the brim of his cap
and gave his lectures a subtle, wild edge?

Perhaps you saw him in some pub corner,
over-pouring sake in a guinomi,
a simple and beautiful thing, a gift
carried from a small fishing village
where summers brought their storms
and a stormbell still rang in August, for the dead.
Pushing the tumbler with gentle ceremony
across the table to no one
and leaving it there to cool
as he unsteadied his way home.
He probably looked like you or me.

HOW TO JUMP OFF A BUILDING

When you lean out, gravity reaching up for you,
your shoes letting go the ledge, remember
how your father used to say,
Trust me—those infallible hands.
Don't look at the sidewalk hedges, the street blurring up,
the bystanders, because they can't help you.
They have only the power to watch,
so for their sakes, don't say anything.
It would be too much, that sound, any sound,
anything more than the image of you.
There would be a moment when silence
was the language of the world.
You might remember stories your grandfather told
about men who knew how to die,
their cliff ascents, their failed chutes,
how if they fell, made no sound.
It was that acceptance of the thing beneath
that always seemed so impossible.
                                    Like that face
in the window as you pass, that stunned look,
reaching to her mouth, touching the pane.
Know that she can't save you,
though she needs to like nothing she's ever felt.
Know that your last seconds will last forever—
you will not die at the concrete,
you will go on living, falling past those windows.
You will live on, in her, every bright blue day like today.

BOUNTY

Mold musk, cedar, moss.
Grizzlies and gulls hawking their fishwares
beyond the break. At my feet,
a century-old depression,
not bear bed as the others.

They dug these for themselves,
Jason says. *Smallpox.*
They would go off into the woods
and dig just enough to lay in, and die.

Cottonwood, devil's club, fiddleheads.
A raven's cacophony.
The forest's language: green,
a lexicon of lusciousness,
the boughs brash with longing:
this one a connoisseur of skin,
that one a bard of frailty, echoing
our contagion, our turbulence.

There were maybe ten thousand
of my people   before.

We resume picking, black chanterelles
and matsutakes, knowing this much
can we offer in debt, this much only:
that we are heady with the bounty of it all—
this slope and its dead, this garden of graves.

STARGAZING

Wind frets and shuffles down its dark halls
and starchoir huddles us on the porch.
Everywhere the night feels like it's falling.

Millennia have not brought us yet the tales
of their deaths, what light is gone,
so distant are some. We are cast away,

unmoored. The night has sown stars
in my father's eyes—
a word might break us,

might build of our relics
kingdoms of air the grass pray in,
our stories read in the gnarled skins of trees,

the petals of our bones carrying us
to the sea, where the moon might come
and touch us with light.

STARGAZING II

When the last of my father's family went
their lonely ways in the land of the dead,
the long evenings shunned him their solace.
I wish we were again in the night's bloom
when he would steal me out to watch the stars.
That one? Crux—the Southern Cross.
That one? Orion. Cassiopeia. Ursa Major...
The Dipper may have been pouring night everywhere.
There was poetry in his breath, his silence.
And he would carry me back to my bed,
star-bathed, and I imagine my mother
came as if my skin was burned
and her hands gently, gently across my brow.

HEIR

It was the field, rock by fucking rock,
hauled fenceward, and the field, finally, fenced
and the tender blessing of their knickering
out there in the grass, the tympani of hooves
flushed from the barn, the moon and shadows
pennons in their nightly cantering.

It was hayrakes tidying the mower rows,
the muscled teens by chugging balers cursing
the dogged days, dreaming scanty-clad river drifts,
heaving horsefeed onto the roving balecarts.

Later the acrid fruit and garden growth
bribed from the deer and bears
with apple husks and squash rinds,
pumpkin skins oozing in the compost.

And the low-tide mussels sunning like butterflies
plucked and broken by gulls from their heights
across the salt-skeined bedrocks, .
the snow waning across the tattered ridges
and cedars playing their shadow theatres
on the mossy skins of stones
and ravens singing old myths and lusting
after salmon eyes in the gasping shallows.

It was the dreaded cellar door,
hay bale hives and gunnysack itch,
potato pile scree in the bins, horse pucks
petrifying in the nightshade stalls,
the shelves specimened with mason jars
like trophies from some orchard apothecary.

It was the twenty below, mice treading
the tunnelled walls with mousely abandon,
wind bawling on the roofcorners,
the ache of coveted window displays,
Sears catalogue fantasies,
everything envied, everything craved.
Through the brittle bones of our want,
these were the kingdoms we wished for.

ICE

Say you came and saw snakes and salamanders
warren beneath snowy chandeliers,
saw rimecrusted paw prints, watched
humus freeze to tires, and heard an ice song,
heard the river purl under us. The habit of snow
is sleep, and you came to love its glass moods,
how sun was shared in a billion blinding pixels.
Say you came to believe you knew something
of us, our history perhaps, the investments
of our lives, legends, the laden hours of rain
and snow, the way we hold our secrets.
Say you learned this: the shave and spray echoes
the rustle of steel tuned to the warmth of knives.
It sings the infallibility of ice, the knowledge
of a razor's need to glide, a stick's need to burn,
as if it all, every sliver of the rink
and every broken player felt the desire
to burn the world down with skates.

ROADKILL

Headlights undressing
the roadsides must surely warn,
fuss the hackles of wolf and lynx,
though never cougar crossing

the engine's Doppler swoon—
still all my nocturnal swerves.
Gravel gutfloats and recurves,
reckless tire tunes,.

bugs blown like foundry sparks
from the shadows, offcast glass
fleshing the light—
what offer of the dark

I've not seen? There, a doe,
dead. Far from thicket.
And her fawn... blind stumble
all it knew, it could not know

I meant it love. I wonder
what stories are told in stag
of the one that held you
like you were his daughter?

DEATH BY CHEVY

No way to tell what type, small, yellow
and mummified to the radiator,
fanned like some fresh-air fossil.
One moment flitting ditch grass,
snapping a lush plague of gnats,
then buoyed over the bank
drafted into the Chevy's grill.
Then the rad's dark warmth
to shuck its weight, leave its
little birdy model, shell, husk.
The tines now a restrack in a field
of smattered bugs, the chevron
a tombstone with no words.
I try carrying on, repairing the headlight,
the deer-damaged rad support,
as if this has not wounded me,
as if I came to a field and a cairn
and knowing the dead, detoured,
offered all my body knew left to do.

BEAR

Her smell gone feral in our senses:
salmon rot and roe hung on her
in her kind's rankest perfume.

Lady bear take our awe, our abandon,
our pulses as praise—for the spawners
returning to their cribs to die,

for dawn cutting the world into haunts
of mountainbone, evergreen,
into glacierback, salmonside, grizzly.

THE CALF

That day the whalers hove stationward
the hawserlines sang and threatened
to tear the bollards down.

Too many tons atow, all their wages wagered
to a man they held their breath for the tethers.
Tenderboats watched in the wake.

The quiet one saw the trailing calf
wallow and dive fluke upheld
one aching heartbreak—and gone.

He knew why a whale would hold this pose
only a second for the whale must
or the beauty might break them.

The calf rolled beneath its dead dame and blew
just beside his skiff and stayed
as if to demand not recourse but reason.

He brushed its back its gnarled dorsal
its side caging a heart he could only imagine.
Who can say what words they shared?

However long their time
between the deep and the dust—that touch
a truce speaking fire in his palm.

ONCE A WHALING STATION

Wind rakes the waves, throttles to a howl.
Whales once ushered salmon here,
crooning their moody music through the murk.
Now only flotsam and birdscat
clothe this beach once blazoned with bone.
'20s émigrés camped here: Chinese, Japanese,
unmixed beyond this blood-wine terroir
where grapples slung the carcasses.
Some carted flensed hunks to the tryworks,
others garbed in the burn-barn's rendering stink
fed the firehouse spines, tarsals, jail-bar ribs.
What must they have sung to while the tedium—
what canted shanties of sharking old seas
to woo their fatigue away?
What songs salted their circadian cores
while they'd knead and unfist around evening fires,
pipe smoke at stars, cinch their blankets closer
at wind bawling in the tree peaks,
the station stones even then forgetting their names?

SINGING TO BONES

Her bleach-wood house bleeds nails,
and the birds besotted with sun
nest in brambles run amuck down the pickets
gauzed in summer chaff like dusty furs.
Her '35 Ford has risen in the arms of alders
to the height of a rusty Jesus.
Generations of game have shied
from her orchard, paid their furtive berths,
taken citizenship in the nation of shadows.
Her husband was mauled there years ago
while she was visiting some church circle
of pie-makers all acluck with gossip.
At first she shot only the bears
and left them on the stoops of the apple roots
grown to hives of bluebottle Rorschach
of scavengers nuzzled to the bone trough,
the feast-hall cloisters of carrion ants.

She thought it brutish and fitting.
Her kills played shadowshows in the orchard alleys.
The years went, the place unboned by foxes,
and once a wolf she swore dripped moon in the grass.
Stoic, haughty and gone. She waited every night
through the lunar quarter and wane and ember.
Everything but the wolf returned.
As all things pass, she passed.
See her watch-chair, her burnished rifle butt,
her door hinges growling in the wind,
rapping at the jambs like knocks at the gate of hate
where the wind was always singing to bones,
the croon of her want, *James, James,*
where are you? And what moon, what moon.

THE SPIT

It was the too-many-eth month of a bad job
the bitterness like a worrystone
so I would lunch on the spit that shepherded kayakers
from the wind's worst teeth and savour the saltlick breeze.
Gulls and their kindred always rushed
all agaggle to fight for my bread bits.
It was never about sating them
tossing scraps disobeying the park signs,
it was soaking in that I held some sway
the way they babbled and waddled their cries
how they came out of the drear and out of the sun,
which they may have thought I was breaking.

THE PULL

Before valley this place was silted bedbottom, ocean-
belly, seagut scoured by beastly crustaceans
of unfathomable origin and destiny, for where
can you find them now but in some stone broken
open? Had you told me this rock would bear
my bones I would have laughed and taken

a piece from your hand and skipped it
across the river to see it return where it came from,
where it belongs, this earth that forgets if it is summit
or sea floor, but basks in starlight and sun,
dying into the bigger body of it all, sunk back, a stone
from some hand, into depths none of us know.

IN THE LANGUAGE OF THE MOUNTAIN

The sun broomed snow into piles
and elders saw each moon pull its brightest tide,
saw the river beacon their salmon home.

The *moon of dances* and *angry moon,*
the *moon of good salmon*
when the river dozes in its algaed flowstones,
when the geese wing over the stubble fields
the hills bruised in early autumn,
when the wolves come piping their sad prayers.

In this place of coming together
the words for the way moss fills the shadows
under the trees do not mean *bow,* not *fall*
on your knees, that is just how they are spoken.

IN THE LANGUAGE OF THE MOUNTAIN II

You might instead of burn
say the garden where you grow flames.

Instead of calling your lover
luster the pearl of their name.

The wind flutters and gusts
like the heart of a wounded bird—

it thithers, it yons, it wanderlusts
because it has no words,

has always known goodbye
as the river's voice, and why

the words for rain, for lichen,
for moss sipping shadows under trees

do not mean *bow*, not *fall on your knees*—
that is just how they are spoken.

SITTING ON A FALLEN CEDAR

It has taught us sway, unsway,
to mimic its crown
browsyful in the banqueting wind.

The last storm laid it down, here,
where dew nests in the grass
like the eyes of a field of serpents.

There must be a word for how light finds one
sitting on a fallen cedar,
the stand in their burled tongue

adding a verse in the dusty croon of us,
the moon candling in the clouds
and wandering through the trees,

everything painted shades of soot
and raven, of obsidian and snakeback,
the wind a suggestion of cello,

the low chorus of rot building, a vigil of ants
marking the mossroot concourse
through lily tongue and hellebore—

if you slow their song, the crickets become
tremulous, vibratory, haunting as a choir
where no choir should be,

where the ants gauge our footfalls,
everything bated,
and as we move, they move.

THE SALMON WORD FOR HOME

What stories would carry from these ruins if words
could echo—our bygones unfurled from the dust
of tattered towns where ruin spread its limbs
and muscled roots, where once
strangers played and swung? We know
by their tools and relics splayed

through strata what nations homed and played
their summers here. There must be a word
the salmon have for *home*, one the nations know
can only be sung where glacierdust
blues the waters of their cribs with what once
was stone. Even cedar limbs

know the simplest communion: all those limbs
bent, as if in blessing. Current played
from the reeds of stones, a flume that once
was ice secreting the winter-croon words
of cirques from the craggy corner dust
across flowstones in a song we all know.

We mark the river's mood: has it known
rain, highwatering the tributary limbs,
or August air christened with hay-rake dust?
From each a verse. Call it summer purl played
in moonlight minor. Or spring's throated foreword
to flood. Tales we've hung on in our once-

upon-a-time ages: rockabye once
more. Will a voice in the dervish know
prayers and pass, and afterward
who will tend the little ones? Storms delimb
saplings and oldgrowth alike, ruin replayed
in motley scapes, rot returning the dust

its tithes. O boghymn, will-o-the-wisp, dost
the fable die with us? Who will tale, once
we're gone, who'll trumpet our downplayed
deeds? How moot. In absence, what is known
of us is token. Rain is prelim
to the river's mood, but it is not an afterword

to the story played—it *is* the story. The salmon word
for home is glacierdust and once-tall trees unlimbed,
a taste, no matter where, they know.

AFTER THIS

Waterscour bowled the granite gorge to cascades
the stream rode like wind over the skin of distant dunes,
carried cutbanks to catchbasins
time alone knows the beginnings of.
Deposits left a dung-washed bluff of bird boreholes
riddled in the sediment lees, and falls swelled by runoff
freighted the air with thunder and mist.
Elders in their fourth score bore legends of such rain—
as if by fingersnap, some unseen broody genesis upcountry
that sent the coon brood clawing for high ground,
a cougar cub snarling its distaste,
birds flushed from their warrens, a rookery of pleas,
the grizzly who would never be there unharried.
The man, too, in a cave too tomblike to forget,
above the floodline, ten feet abreast of his bear,
listening to the hullsong of stones shunting through the gorge,
the storm's hooves commanding them to sit
and watch, and learn how to live after this.

One more coin
in the bank of beautiful sins.

—Robert Wrigley

NOTES

Marakuja from "In Praise of Pain" is a passion fruit in Swahili.

The lines "Let us open the mud book and pray" ("In Praise of Mud") and "Sleeping peacefully in the kingdom of agony" ("In the Kingdom of Agony") are shamelessly stolen from Robert Wrigley and Philip Levine, respectively.

The women dancing out to the birds in "The Church of a Barn's Shadow" are doing the *zapateo*, the fiery, rhythmic foot stomping of flamenco.

"The Bone Temple" was inspired by Kutná Hora in the Czech Republic.

The title "Parents Waiting for Waves to Return Kids" was taken from an AP headline.

"How to Carry a Cross" is inspired by a story John Dickinson told years ago. He had that professor, yes, who had recommended the only two cities to be atomically bombed. His imagining is all mine, down to the guinomi, his simple ceramic sake tumbler. It all seemed too much for one man to carry.

ACKNOWLEDGMENTS

My endless thanks to the editors who gave these poems homes:

The Antietam Review: "Bone Lullabies"

The Baltimore Review: "Sitting on a Fallen Cedar" and "Heir"

Cascadia Review: "Tree of Life" and "After This"

Clackamas Literary Review: "How to Jump off a Building" and "Singing to Bones"

Diagram: "Death by Chevy"

Event: "The Calf"

The Fiddlehead: "In Praise of the Village Idiot," "Sand" and "Thunder Eggs"

Forget Magazine: "Roadkill" and "Stargazing II"

Gargoyle: "The Bone Temple" and "Ornithos"

Good Foot: "In Praise of Pain"

Literary Review of Canada: "Lucky"

The Malahat Review: "In Praise of Mud"

Mid-American Review: "How to Be Eaten by a Lion" and "The Volcanologist's Lament"

The Nashwaak Review: "Parents Waiting for Waves to Return Kids"

The New Formalist: "The Horologist's Lament"

Nimrod: "How to Carry a Cross"

The Pedestal Magazine: "Ice," "Vengeance" (as "Bread of Vengeance") and "Death by Lightning" (as "The Story of Lightning")

Poetry East: "The Church of Rot" and "The Volcanologist's Lament II"

PRISM International: "Hell," "In the Language of the
Mountain" and "Rainmaker"

Queen's Quarterly: "The Church of Steel" and "Murder"

Spillway: "Bear"

Shenandoah: "Democracy" and "Dew"

Talking River Review: "In the Kingdom of Agony"
(Reprinted in *Talking River* 2004)

Valparaiso Poetry Review: "Once a Whaling Station"

Weber: "Bounty," "How Water Works," "The Church of
Purslane and Primrose," "The Pull," "The Salmon
Word for Home" and "Stargazing"

"How to Be Eaten by a Lion" appeared in *The Best American
Poetry 2009*.

"The Church of Steel" appeared in *The Best Canadian Poetry
in English 2009*.

"In Praise of the Village Idiot" appeared in *The Best
Canadian Poetry in English 2010*.

"The Salmon Word for Home" and "Stargazing" received the
2014 Dr. Sherwin Howard Award for Best Poetry from
Weber: The Contemporary West.

"Ornithos," "Once a Whaling Station," "Tree of Life," "The
Church of My Mother's Hands," "After This" and
"Lucky" were nominated for the 2008 Bronwen Wallace
Award for Emerging Writers from the Writer's Trust of
Canada.

The epigraph from Robert Hass is from "Songs to Survive
the Summer" in *The Apple Trees at Olema*, and that
from Robert Wrigley is from "Angels" in *In the Bank of
Beautiful Sins*.

For the faith and kindness, the patience and friendship:
Thank you to every one my wonderful teachers, especially
Kim Barnes and Bob Wrigley, Jason Fales and Dennis Held.
To friends old and new who read and helped and offered of
themselves and made my work better, lest I forget any, believe
me, thank you all. To my family for putting up with me, for
encouraging me. To my mentor, old friend, Claire Davis, all
these words are thanks. And to Silas White, this book truly
wouldn't be here without you—I can't thank you enough.

ABOUT THE AUTHOR

Michael Johnson's work has appeared in numerous literary journals including *The Antigonish Review, The Fiddlehead, The Malahat Review, PRISM International, Mid-American Review* and *Gargoyle*. He was a finalist for *Poetry* magazine's Ruth Lilly Fellowship and the Bronwen Wallace Award for Emerging Writers. He was nominated for the Pushcart Prize and, in 2014, won the Dr. Sherwin W. Howard Award for best poetry in *Weber: The Contemporary West*. He lives in Penticton, BC.

PHOTO CREDIT: KASHKA CLELLAMIN